W9-BAN-896

CHRISTMAS
IN WILLIAMSBURG

300 Years of Family Traditions

By K. M. Kostyal
with
Colonial Williamsburg®
THE COLONIAL WILLIAMSBURG FOUNDATION

PHOTOGRAPHY BY LORI EPSTEIN

NATIONAL
GEOGRAPHIC
WASHINGTON, D.C.

TABLE OF CONTENTS

Introduction: An Evolving Holiday   10

CHRISTMAS PAST   12
Christmas in Early America • 1600s   14
Christmas Is Come • 1700s   16
     HEARTY HOT CHOCOLATE   19
     BOXING DAY   23
     SPICING UP THE HOLIDAYS   24
A Victorian Christmas • 1800s   26
     CHRISTMAS CAROLING   30
     PAPER CHAINS   32

CHRISTMAS PRESENT   34
A Town and Season Reborn • 1900s   36
     GINGERBREAD HOUSES   39
Christmas Now • Present Time   40
     SETTING A COLONIAL TABLE   43
     TREE TAGS   47
     12TH NIGHT CAKE   48
     DECORATE YOUR OWN WREATH   50

Conclusion: An American Christmas   52
Festive Recipes   54
Christmas Time Line   56
Resources   58
Index   59

LEFT: Every year the Christmas tree at the Williamsburg Inn is filled with elegant decorations in the Regency style, popular in the early 1800s.

An Evolving HOLiDAY

THE TRADITIONS THAT MAKE CHRISTMAS such a special holiday for us aren't really very old. Everybody knows that for Christians, Christmas is a celebration of the birth of Jesus Christ. But for most of the 2,000 years since he was born, there were no celebrations of that day—in fact, his birth date may not even have been December 25.

That day may have been chosen for the "Christ Mass" because it fell near the darkest part of the year and the shortest day of the year—the winter solstice. Before Christianity became widespread in northern Europe, a lot of "pagan" religions decorated with evergreen and holly branches and lit fires to welcome back the sun in the days after the solstice had passed. To the Druids, who were priests in western Europe at about the time Jesus was born, nothing was more sacred than the mistletoe. In much later centuries, the English decorated homes and taverns with mistletoe, but by then it wasn't seen as sacred. Instead, it was an invitation to people standing under sprigs to kiss.

When the first colonists arrived in America in the 1600s, they brought with them some of the English Yuletide traditions, but they adapted them to the New World. For the people of Williamsburg and the rest of Virginia, December 25 was a holy day marked by going to church, but it was also the beginning of the Twelve Days of Christmas. It was a time filled with dancing, feasting, and fox hunting—for those who could afford it—but not much gift giving.

It really wasn't until the 1800s that a lot of our current Christmas traditions came to America. In 1823 the long-robed St. Nicholas—a fourth-century bishop and the patron saint of children—was turned into a jolly, pink-cheeked elf in "A Visit from St. Nicholas," a poem that became very popular. In that night before Christmas there were Christmas stockings but no tree. That was soon to come.

In Williamsburg a professor from Germany was the first to introduce the idea of decorating a tree, in 1842. His was so small it could sit on top of a table. But as the 19th century went on, Santa Claus, Christmas trees, cards, carols, and families gathered together for cozy holidays became part of the holiday celebrations.

Every new wave of immigrants coming from Europe to America brought their own Christmas music, food, and ways of giving and receiving. And in Williamsburg, the old colonial traditions were combined with new ones that evolved after the town was restored in the 1930s. Now front doors are decorated with imaginative wreaths, and a Grand Illumination celebrated with fireworks in early December marks the beginning of a season that still warms the heart, as enduring as family and friends and the delights of tradition.

BELOW: Colonial Williamsburg's historic homes are famous for outdoor decorations made of natural materials such as fruit and evergreen leaves. Pineapples, which many today think of as a symbol of hospitality, are often part of Christmas arrangements.

CHRISTMAS PAST

Colonial families and friends gathered for long visits during the Twelve Days of Christmas. The big midday meal included many meats, wild fowl, game, and sweets.

*The extreame winde, rayne,
frost and snow caused us to keep
Christmas among the Salvages.*

—John Smith, 1608

Christmas in Early
AMERICA

THE FIRST VIRGINIA COLONISTS who settled Jamestown were too busy trying to survive to give much thought to Christmas. In 1608, the beginning of their second winter, they were starving. So a group of men led by Capt. John Smith set out in a boat to barter with the chief of the Powhatan Indians for food. A storm stopped them, and Smith and some of the men spent days with the Indians at the Kecoughtan village. Smith wrote about his "Christmas among the Salvages, where we were never more merrie, nor fedde on more plentie of good oysters, fish, flesh, wild foule, and good bread; nor never had better fires in England, then in the drie warme smokie houses of the Kecoughtan."

The Puritans who settled New England didn't believe in a merry Christmas. They thought it shouldn't be observed at all, and they had laws to punish anyone who did. But as the Virginia colony became better established, people began to celebrate more. In December, with the harvest over, there was time for visiting other farms and plantations. Like John Smith in the "smokie houses of Kecoughtan," Virginians feasted on the bounty of the land and the fields and made merry.

LEFT: An artist captures the piety of the New England Pilgrims who settled Plimoth Plantation in 1620. They did not believe in celebrating Christmas at all, and one of them recalled that "On the day called Christmas Day, the Governor called them out to work…"

Now Christmas is come,
'tis fit that we
Should feast and sing,
and merry be...

—*Virginia Almanack, 1765*

CHRISTMAS
Is Come

LEFT: The Christmas feasts kept women busy, especially enslaved African-Virginians. In the 1700s, long before electricity was available, cooking, cleaning up, and keeping fires stoked with wood meant long, hard hours in the kitchen.

IMAGINE A LAND SLICED BY RIVERS and creeks, where the towns were few and far between, and most people were farmers. The wealthy gentry owned huge plantations worked by enslaved black people, but most farmers had much less land, and the crops they grew fed their own families. Still, this place, this colony of Virginia, was a land of plenty. The rivers were full of fish, oysters, clams, ducks, and geese, and the woods full of deer, turkeys, and partridges.

From spring till late in the fall, everyone's attention was focused on the growing season. But by December the harvest was in, and people could relax a little.

In the colonial capital of Williamsburg and across Virginia, the excitement began to build as the month went on. The Twelve Days of Christmas were about to begin for everyone. "Nothing is to be heard of in conversation, but the balls, the fox hunts, the fine entertainments, and the good fellowship which are to be exhibited at the approaching Christmas," wrote a young man named Philip Fithian. A tutor at one of the large plantations, Fithian kept a journal recording his life in colonial Virginia.

At the College of William & Mary, which sat at one end of Williamsburg's main street, Duke of Gloucester, the boys began to be more restless than usual. It was time for the holidays to begin, and they were getting up their nerve for the annual "bar out." One day soon, when their instructor would try to come into the classroom, they'd bar the door with their bodies, keeping him out and announcing loud and clear that it was time for their annual winter break. It was all in fun; most things were in this season.

TOP: Young students at the College of William & Mary "bar out" their instructor from the classroom, a custom that announced it was time for the holiday break. Not just for older boys, the college also taught young teenagers in the colonial period.

The first sign of the festivities was on Christmas Eve, when guns were fired into the chill Virginia air. The next day, Christmas, was a quiet holy day marked by going to church, where a few sprigs of holly in the deep windowsills were the only decorations for the season. When Fithian was living in western Virginia, he noted in his journal, "To Day is like other Days every Way calm & temperate—People go about their daily Business."

LEFT: On Christmas Eve, musket shots, fired in celebration, rang in the Twelve Days of Christmas.

Hearty Hot Chocolate

Kids rarely got to taste chocolate in colonial Virginia. People thought of it as a stimulant for adults, and hot chocolate made with either milk, water, or wine was a favorite drink in coffeehouses like R. Charlton's. Here's a recipe for one kind of hot chocolate colonial Virginians drank. It's a simpler version of the kind Frank Clark of Colonial Williamsburg's Historic Foodways department (right) makes in the Governor's Palace kitchen with authentic colonial cooking utensils.

4 ounces bittersweet chocolate with
70–80 percent cocoa
2 cups milk or table cream or a combination
sugar to taste

Grate the chocolate from the chocolate bar. Then heat the milk and cream. To get the foamy top the colonialists liked, hold a whisk vertically in the pot and rub your palms together rapidly with the whisk handle beween them. That creates the action of an 18th-century chocolate mill. Add the chocolate and continue to whisk gently as the chocolate melts. If you like your hot chocolate less thick, add more milk or cream, then sugar to taste, starting with about 1½ teaspoons per cup. Let it cool a little before sipping, then enjoy!

But this was just the beginning. In Williamsburg and in the scattered plantations across eastern Virginia, relatives and friends had come for long visits of weeks, even months. The women and the house servants were busy planning and preparing great feasts full of the land's bounty—20 or 30 different dishes carefully arranged on the table for the big afternoon meal. Each dish was offset by another across the table from it, because from architecture to gardens to food, colonial Virginians liked symmetry.

At the grand balls of the gentry, endless desserts were served around midnight, after hours of dancing. One girl from the gentry wrote in her diary that "on thursday the 26th of decem. Mama made 6 mince pies & 7 custards, 12 tarts, 1 chicking pye, and 4 puddings for the ball." Hostesses also pleased the eyes and palates of their guests with "dessert pyramids" of carefully stacked apples and pears or small cakes and mince pies.

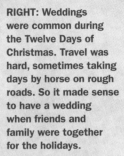

Eating and dancing were what the Twelve Days of Christmas were all about. Virginians loved to dance, everything from formal minuets to country dances. Our young friend Fithian recorded a full day of dancing, beginning after breakfast, with a break for afternoon dinner, then continuing until "it grew too dark to dance."

With everyone gathered together and in festive spirits, this was also a good time for weddings. In fact, two Virginia gentlemen who would become Founding Fathers of the nation married their wives during the Christmas holidays: George Washington and Thomas Jefferson.

While the elaborate balls and feasts were something only the gentry could afford, most other white colonists ate well and made merry. But what about the many enslaved black people? By the mid-1700s there were more of them in Williamsburg than there were white people. And all year the slaves worked hard, whether they lived on the large plantations

RIGHT: Weddings were common during the Twelve Days of Christmas. Travel was hard, sometimes taking days by horse on rough roads. So it made sense to have a wedding when friends and family were together for the holidays.

BOTTOM: After the wedding ceremony, the dancing began. Virginians loved the minuet, the reel, and other popular dances of the period.

INSET: Colorful kissing balls, now a part of a Williamsburg Christmas, were unknown to colonial Virginians, as were a lot of our holiday traditions.

or small farms or in the Williamsburg homes of the gentry and the "middling sort," the merchants and craftsmen who had enough money to own slaves and enjoy a better life.

Whatever holiday celebrations the African-Virginians had were simple, their cooking pots probably full of food such as wild game and root vegetables. But despite the simplicity of what they ate, this was probably a comparatively happy time for many of them because they were allowed to visit with friends and family who belonged to other owners.

Historians think the enslaved people who worked in the farm fields were given a few days off during the Christmas season, but they don't know how house slaves were treated during the long holidays. Their hands and skills were needed to cook and serve and clean. It must have been a particularly busy time for them, with constant meals to prepare and guests to take care of. Still, just like the enslaved people who worked in the fields, most would have been given the gift of a few coins in acknowledgment of the holiday.

TOP: During the holidays enslaved African-Virginians might be allowed by their owners to visit relatives living nearby. For some, this was the only time of year they saw their mothers and fathers, or sons and daughters.

BOTTOM:
An early American wooden rocking horse.

RIGHT: The Virginia gentry enjoyed fox hunting during the long holidays. Hounds would follow the scent of a fox and lead riders on horseback to the cornered animal.

As for the young children of the white colonists, on New Year's Day they might also have been given a few coins or an educational book, even a small toy. And schoolboys sometimes wrote a Christmas "piece" for their parents during the holidays. These weren't really holiday greetings; they were more a way to show off good penmanship. Gift giving just wasn't a big part of the season yet. The Twelve Days of Christmas were really a time for adults, not children. But in the century to come, things began to change.

BOXING DAY

In countries around the world December 26 is celebrated as Boxing Day, a day of goodwill. The name comes from a tradition dating to the 1700s in England, when servants were given small ceramic boxes with coins (or pieces of coins, such as the ones below) in them on the day after Christmas. Today many people around the world still give small gifts on Boxing Day, often money, to those who've helped them during the year. You can come up with your own ways of celebrating Boxing Day. Perhaps box up your old clothes, books, and toys for charity. Or make a list of the people who help you all year—teachers, crossing guards, cleaning staff—and create simple gifts to give them next time you see them. Cookies or nuts are always welcomed. To add to the Boxing Day tradition, put your gifts in small hand-decorated cardboard boxes and explain that your present is a custom from this centuries-old holiday.

Spicing UP the Holiday

One thing about the colonial era: It didn't really smell very good. Lots of things scented the air, including pig manure and horse dung, since people and livestock shared the town. Humans in the past had a clever way to keep from smelling the bad odors. They made pomanders to sniff, so they'd smell something nice instead. Here's how to make your own pomander to sniff or to hang as a spicy holiday decoration. It's especially fun to do this with a friend or family member.

6 When you've finished decorating your orange, tie a ribbon around your creation and enjoy the spicy smell of Christmas past.

24

1 You'll need a nice round, medium-size orange, about 2 cups of cloves, a colorful Christmas ribbon about a half inch wide, and something sharp to poke holes in the orange. An awl, a bamboo skewer, or the point of a fork will work. If you want to hang your pomander, you'll also need some thin wire or nylon fishing line to suspend it.

2 Now the fun begins. Hold the orange in one hand and stick a hole in it with your sharp tool. Next put a clove in the hole.

3 Stick another hole for a clove in the orange, about a fingertip's width away from the first hole, fill with a clove, and do the same again. After three cloves you can probably tell how hard or easy this is going to be for you.

4 Now that you've gotten the hang of it, it's time to decide on a design, and that depends on how many cloves you want to stick in. You could make clove outlines of circles or stars or butterflies or any other simple design you like.

5 Or you can make a real colonial pomander and cover the whole surface of the orange with cloves. That takes a lot of cloves and time, but you'll have a great-smelling pomander that will last for months.

25

The children were nestled all snug in their beds,
While visions of sugar-plums danced in their heads.
—"The Night Before Christmas," 1823

A Victorian CHRISTMAS

BY THE 1800S, Americans weren't colonists anymore but citizens of an independent new nation. Life was changing for the former colonists, and so was Christmas. Immigrants from other European countries kept pouring in, bringing their Christmas customs with them. Germans especially loved to celebrate Christmas, and one of their traditions was to cut a small evergreen tree, set it up in their homes, and decorate it with real candles clipped to the branches!

In Williamsburg, the first Christmas tree was introduced to the town by Charles Minnigerode, a professor teaching at the College of William & Mary. One of the many refugees who had fled the political turbulence in Europe during the mid-1800s, Minnigerode boarded with the Tucker family on Nicholson Street. In 1842, he delighted the Tucker children by showing them how to set up a little evergreen tree on a table in the parlor and decorate it with gilded nuts, paper cutouts, and candles. "Supreme excitement reigned in the Tucker family on that Christmas Day," a visiting relative recalled many years later. "Other children of the

LEFT: The famous 19th-century illustrator Thomas Nast popularized the image of Santa Claus as a jolly, bearded, rotund fellow.

27

neighborhood were invited in, and they danced and shouted as the candles were lit one by one…When the tree had been admired and Christmas gifts exchanged, the older people led the young in singing hymns and carols."

Christmas was on its way to becoming America's most important holiday, far different from the kind of midwinter festival, full of adult dancing and feasting, that it had been during the colonial era. It was becoming much more of a family holiday and a time that excited every child.

What, of course, excited them most, was a visit from a round, jolly fellow in a red suit, made famous by a poem

ABOVE: The children in the St. George Tucker House in Williamsburg were delighted when, in 1842, Charles Minnigerode introduced them to a custom from his native Germany: decorating a small tree for Christmas. It was the first the town had ever seen.

ABOVE: The 1823 poem
known as "The Night
Before Christmas" is
still cherished today.

RIGHT: In 1897 this
now famous letter first
appeared in the *New
York Sun* newspaper.

Is There a Santa Claus?

We take pleasure in answering at once
and thus prominently the communication
below, expressing at the same time our
great gratification that its faithful author
is numbered among the friends of THE SUN:

"DEAR EDITOR: I am 8 years old.

"Some of my little friends say there is no Santa
Claus.

"Papa says 'If you see it in THE SUN it's so.'

"Please tell me the truth; is there a Santa Claus?

"VIRGINIA O'HANLON.

"115 WEST NINETY-FIFTH STREET."

VIRGINIA, your little friends are wrong.
They have been affected by the skepticism
of a skeptical age. They do not believe
except they see. They think that nothing
can be which is not comprehensible by
their little minds. All minds, VIRGINIA,
whether they be men's or children's, are
little. In this great universe of ours man
is a mere insect, an ant, in his intellect, as
compared with the boundless world about
him, as measured by the intelligence capa-
ble of grasping the whole of truth and
knowledge.

Yes, VIRGINIA, there is a Santa Claus.
He exists as certainly as love and generosity and devotion exist, and you know that
they abound and give to your life its high-
est beauty and joy. Alas! how dreary
would be the world if there were no Santa
Claus. It would be as dreary as if there
were no VIRGINIAS. There would be no
childlike faith then, no poetry, no romance
to make tolerable this existence. We
should have no enjoyment, except in sense
and sight. The eternal light with which
childhood fills the world would be ex-
tinguished.

Not believe in Santa Claus! You might
as well not believe in fairies! You might
get your papa to hire men to watch in all
the chimneys on Christmas Eve to catch
Santa Claus, but even if they did not see
Santa Claus coming down, what would that
prove? Nobody sees Santa Claus, but that
is no sign that there is no Santa Claus.
The most real things in the world are those
that neither children nor men can see. Did
you ever see fairies dancing on the lawn?
Of course not, but that's no proof that they
are not there. Nobody can conceive or
imagine all the wonders there are unseen
and unseeable in the world.

You may tear apart the baby's rattle and
see what makes th...

29

we now know as "The Night Before Christmas." It appeared anonymously in 1823 in the *Troy Sentinel*, an upstate New York newspaper, but it was later attributed to Clement Clarke Moore, a professor in New York City. Some scholars now wonder if Moore really was the author, but whoever wrote it, the poem—with its dancing sugarplums, stockings hung by the fire, and elfish St. Nicholas driving eight tiny reindeer—charmed America.

CHRISTMAS Caroling

Even though colonial Virginians loved dancing and making music during the holiday season, historians can't find any diaries or other sources that say they had special music for that time of year. But in England, France, and Germany, Christmas music was popular in the 1700s. Some of the hymns we know today, including "Hark the Herald Angels Sing" and "Oh, Come All Ye Faithful," were written then.

After the Revolutionary War, composers in America also began publishing Christmas songs, and it was probably in the 1800s during the Victorian era that small groups of people began going door to door, serenading neighbors with their singing. That caroling tradition has its roots in an old English custom called wassailing that dates back to the Middle Ages. Then, the groups of singers were often given something to eat or drink (including a spicy punch also called wassail) as a way to thank them for their music.

You've probably heard carolers or been caroling yourself. If not, it's easy to do. Just invite friends, family, and neighbors to sing familiar carols at homes on your block. Make sure you include the song "Here We Come A-wassailing." The chorus has a nice holiday message:

> *Love and joy come to you,*
> *And to you your wassail too;*
> *And God bless you and send you*
> *A happy New Year.*

As the century went on and war again overtook the country—this time a civil war—America needed charming and cheering. In 1862, the war came to Williamsburg, and a battle raged just outside the town. In December of that same year, a cartoonist named Thomas Nast recalled the legendary St. Nicholas of his native Germany and drew a picture of him giving gifts to Union soldiers for *Harper's Weekly* magazine. When the war ended and the mood of the country lifted, Nast's drawings of the elf saint became more and more cheerful, until they embodied the chubby-cheeked, twinkle-eyed Santa Claus we know today.

ABOVE: This Victorian Santa ingeniously clips to the Christmas tree branch.

WHILE CAROLS AND TREES and Santa all became part of Christmas for Americans during the 19th century, so did something a bit more elusive—the "spirit" of Christmas, a spirit of well-wishing and hope and generosity. And that spirit was at the very heart of a tale told by a popular English writer. Beginning in the 1830s, Charles Dickens wrote a Christmas story every year, a story that all of Britain looked forward to. This was a time when the British people, like Americans, were beginning to celebrate Christmas with more traditions and to long for the festive spirit of Christmases past. In 1843, just a year after Minnigerode set up his tree in Williamsburg and the same year the first commercial Christmas cards were published, Dickens's annual holiday story, *A Christmas Carol,* was published. In Dickens's "carol," the mean and miserly Ebenezer Scrooge is visited by the ghosts of Christmas Past, Present, and Future, and what they show him opens his heart to the true spirit of Christmas—a spirit of goodwill toward all.

In Williamsburg, Christmas past and Christmas present have melded their traditions to create a spirit unique to a town that has celebrated the season and its delights for 300 years.

Paper Chains

Paper chains have been a popular way to decorate for a long time. Colonial Virginians draped their dinner tables with paper chains. And the first Christmas tree in Williamsburg, put up in 1842, had paper chains as part of its decorations. One like it (below) is still decorated in the St. George Tucker House. Make your own paper chains to decorate a Christmas tree or table or to drape around doors or even your bedroom furniture. They'll add a merry spirit wherever you put them.

1 You'll need a ruler with a metal edge running down the length of it, glue, a glue brush, and heavy colorful paper (marbleized paper makes a nice chain). To make marbleized paper, start with white paper, color it with fingerpaints, then wiggle a design in it with a comb. If you want to be really authentic and use the kind of glue Virginians used in the past, mix one part flour to six parts water. Boil that for 20 minutes, then let it cool.

2 You're ready to begin. So first lay a ruler down the length of one sheet of paper, about a half inch from the edge.

3 Beginning at the top, carefully pull the half-inch strip down toward the bottom.

4 Put a little glue on one of the ends of the colored side of the strip.

5 With the colored part of the paper on the outside, make a circle and attach the glue end to the other end. Then pull down another strip and loop it through the opening in your first circle before you glue it, so you can start forming a chain. You can make your chain as long or as short as you like. Use your imagination and mix different colors and designs of paper. You could even write messages on some of the strips. Have fun inventing all kinds of paper chains.

33

The sounds of fife and drum lilt through Colonial Williamsburg's Historic Area as the costumed "militia" marches through town.

CHRISTMAS PRESENT

"How delighted Charles Dickens
would be with these Virginians."

—Scottish bishop on a Christmas visit
   to Virginia, 1927

A Town and Season
REBORN

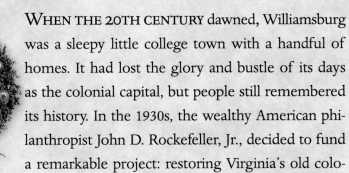

WHEN THE 20TH CENTURY dawned, Williamsburg was a sleepy little college town with a handful of homes. It had lost the glory and bustle of its days as the colonial capital, but people still remembered its history. In the 1930s, the wealthy American philanthropist John D. Rockefeller, Jr., decided to fund a remarkable project: restoring Virginia's old colonial capital, building by building, so that it would recapture the way life had been in the 1700s.

Restoring Williamsburg was a massive job that involved scholars, architects, and craftsmen—and it's still going on today. But in the 1930s, the experts were just beginning this process and local people were so enthusiastic about it that they added their own personal touches. In their zeal, they wanted Christmas to reflect the spirit of the holiday as they knew it, not necessarily as it had been celebrated by their colonial predecessors—which, in truth, was nothing like the 20th-century holiday.

The century before, Christmas decorations had become a big part of the season, with holly and evergreen boughs bedecking doors and windows and the inside of homes.

LEFT: The "Williamsburg look"—doors festooned with wreaths and garlands—became fashionable across America in the mid-20th century.

As Williamsburg was being restored, the townswomen brought their talent for this kind of decorating to new heights. One of the women even went to the Library of Congress in Washington, D.C., to research how the colonial Virginians decorated for Christmas. She couldn't find any historical documents about colonial holiday decorations at all. Despite that, many of Williamsburg's women began to create elaborate wreaths for their front doors and tabletop arrangements of fruits, nuts, and evergreens. They even held contests to compete for the best decorations. Their artistry attracted more and more visitors, who came to enjoy the "Williamsburg Christmas look." Across America, people tried to copy that look in their own homes.

In truth, of course, the "Williamsburg look" had nothing at all to do with the colonial period. Except for a few sprigs of holly on the windowsills of Bruton Parish Church and maybe tucked behind picture frames in homes, Virginians in the 1700s didn't decorate. Besides, fruits like pineapples and oranges were imported treats that would never have been wasted on an outdoor wreath. Nor did colonial Virginians have Christmas trees filled with glittering ornaments and colored lights as a blazing centerpiece in their homes. But this kind of historical accuracy wasn't yet part of the thinking of the townspeople. Like the historians working on the restoration, they were learning how to interpret the past and live in this resurrected town as they went along.

In 1935, with just five buildings restored, one candle was placed in each window of the buildings and lit every night during Christmas week. Residents were asked to do the same in their own homes, but burning real candles was time-consum-

TOP: In the restored town of Williamsburg, costumed interpreters, some of them children, re-create life here in the 18th century. These girls are playing with the kind of doll that would have been popular in the colonial era.

BOTTOM: A single white candle.

ing, expensive, and dangerous, so most people didn't bother. Then in 1934, electric candles became available, and Williamsburg had its first White Lighting. House by house, windows winked awake with the bloom of a single white candle.

Over the years, the White Lighting became the Grand Illumination. Fife and drum corps paraded down Duke of Gloucester to welcome in the season, fireworks pierced the air, and the Williamsburg holiday season became a month-long celebration of both the past and the present. From around the country, and the world, visitors flooded in to see the colonial town that had been reborn—and with it a Christmas unlike any other ever celebrated before or since.

Gingerbread HOUSES

For 40 years now, Colonial Williamsburg's chefs have been making gingerbread houses (such as the gingerbread Governor's Palace below) and even whole villages that are works of art. "In the 19th century, gingerbread houses became romanticized and modernized," pastry chef Rodney Diehl explains. "This was during the time of the *Grimms' Fairy Tales*. So, many of the designs of gingerbread houses actually retain a fantasy appeal." His team starts planning the theme of their gingerbread creations in the summer and making them long before they go on display.

If you want to make your own house—or village—try a colonial theme. You could model yours after the one below or use the colonial house pictures on pages 36 or 45 to guide you. Start with the gingerbread house dough recipe on page 56 for the walls, then be inventive with your decorations—candy canes, pieces of hard candy, and cinnamon sticks work well.

Diehl suggests using shredded wheat and Necco Wafers for roofs, licorice sticks to outline, and powdered sugar for snow. You can make people and animals from marzipan or gingerbread. You can even add small wreaths and swags of real spruce or another soft evergreen.

Something about an old-fashioned
Christmas is hard to forget.

—Hugh Downs, American broadcaster

CHRISTMAS
Now

STROLL DOWN DUKE OF GLOUCESTER Street on a chilly late afternoon in December today, and you will find a small colonial town darkening into a Virginia night. The smell of gingerbread cookies scents the air, and when the sun sets, the piping of fifes and the beating of drums drift closer as a band of musicians marches by. Next the street settles into a hushed quiet as cresset baskets filled with bright-burning pine are set aglow and white lights wink on in windows of restored homes. Diners retreat to welcoming tavern rooms, where they can try colonial specialties such as corn chowder or game "pye," all topped off with a frothy-sweet syllabub. Serving women in ankle-length skirts and mop caps and serving men in knee breeches add their own spark to the colonial atmosphere.

After dinner, families walk through the peaceful darkness of the Palace Green to the imposing Governor's Palace itself, where blazing candles and chamber music or dancing recall colonial revelries. There are more musical offerings at the colonial Courthouse and the Capitol, and the streets begin to bustle again as groups set off on "ghost walks," in search of

LEFT: Every year, fireworks light up the night during the Grand Illumination, heralding the Christmas season. Music throughout the town and candles winking in the windows of historic homes add to this festive evening in early December.

spirits still lingering from the past—convicted pirates, accused witches, or just colonials who find it hard to leave the world they knew—and the holiday traditions they loved.

In Colonial Williamsburg that world is still alive and well. The scene in the restored buildings reflects the love of food and entertaining those early Virginians celebrated during the Twelve Days of Christmas, and costumed interpreters re-create both the festiveness and the hard work that went into the long holiday season. Dining tables are carefully set with 18th-century feasts, prepared according to recipes from the period. Since 1984, Colonial Williamsburg has had a Historic Foodways program to research exactly what and how Virginians ate. The Christmas tables are now filled with the wild game and farm-raised meats, vegetables, and sweets from a time past. Each dish is arranged opposite another one, or

BELOW: At Bassett Hall, reenactors decorate a tree in the Colonial Revival style of the 1940s. This house was where John D. Rockefeller, Jr., the philanthropist who funded Williamsburg's restoration, stayed during the 1930s and '40s.

SETTING a Colonial TABLE

I n 18th-century Williamsburg, people loved symmetry—in their home designs, in their garden designs, even in the way they set their tables. If they put a serving dish on one side of the table, they would place a dish of about the same size on the other, to balance the pattern. The placement of the dishes made a kind of design on the table, and the dishes themselves were a celebration of Virginia's bounty. During the Twelve Days of Christmas, a hostess brought out her finest serving dishes and crystal, and the midday feast featured wild turkeys, ducks, and venison, hams, roast beef, chicken, fish, and oysters, and a few preserved vegetables from local gardens.

And then there were the desserts served after the huge feast, or else set out on a dessert table in the evenings, to be eaten after the dancing was done. All kinds of pies, cakes, small cakes (what we call cookies), fresh fruits, and sweetmeats (candied fruits and nuts, marzipans, and jellies) were symmetrically arranged. Fruits, cookies, and tarts could be carefully stacked into pyramids, and sweetmeats might be served in glass dishes and placed on a tiered glass stand (right). By custom an orange always crowned the arrangement.

Have fun making symmetrical displays and dessert pyramids to celebrate the bounty of your own holiday table—and don't forget to top things off with an orange!

LEFT: Performances on an armonica, a musical instrument invented by Benjamin Franklin, are given every year during Christmas. Glass circles turned by a spinning wheel create its crystalline sound.

ABOVE: Dancing, a favorite holiday pastime with 18th-century Virginians, still shakes the floors in taverns and other historic buildings in Williamsburg.

TOP RIGHT: Light shines from the windows of homes along the historic streets of Williamsburg, and no sounds of traffic mar the mood of a town where the 18th century still lives on.

displayed in a colonial epergne, a tiered glass centerpiece holding lots of smaller dishes. Handmade paper chains drape tables and dessert pyramids of tarts or cookies or fruit pyramids of apples, pineapples, lemons, and oranges provide color to the rather colorless colonial cuisine. Except for those touches, there are no decorations inside most historic buildings, since there would have been none in colonial times.

WILLIAMSBURG'S HISTORY, of course, reaches beyond the colonial era into the centuries that followed, and to honor that rich past, more recent traditions are also part of Christmas present. In the parlor of the old St. George Tucker House on Nicholson Street, a little evergreen ringed with paper chains and hung with gilded nuts and candles sits atop a table, recalling the town's first Christmas tree, decorated in 1842. At the Abby Aldrich Rockefeller Folk Art Museum, a huge tree displays ornaments handmade from gingerbread dough, corncobs, nuts, and other materials that people in the past used to fashion

45

LEFT: Every year, in a parlor of the Williamsburg Inn, guests are invited to write their own wishes on tags and hang them on a Christmas tree.

their decorations. Down the street, the grand evergreen in the Williamsburg Inn drips with elegant gold tassels, swags, medallions, and dried flower ovals, all done in the same Regency style of the inn's decor. Another, smaller tree at the inn reflects a tradition begun about 50 years ago, when visitors were invited to write their own hopes and greetings on small paper tags and hang them on the tree.

For decades, guests at the Williamsburg Inn have written their thoughts of goodwill and thankfulness on small cards and hung them on an inn Christmas tree (left). The messages say everything from "Peace on Earth" to "In Memory of Grandma." It's easy to make your own Christmas tags and invite your guests to add their messages to your tree. The tags become simple, heart-felt reminders of what you and your family and friends really care about. You'll need:

*3 or 4 sheets of a slightly stiff paper in green
    and white*
Scissors
Very narrow red-and-gold ribbon
Something to punch a small, clean hole in the paper
Writing pen

Cut the green paper into two-inch by six-inch rectangles and fold them in half vertically. The folded side is the bottom, and the open end is the top. Punch two holes in the folded paper at the top near the edges on either side, and pull a piece of narrow ribbon through the holes. Tie the two ends of the narrow ribbon together tightly, so they form a secure loop to hook over a branch of the Christmas tree. This is your tree tag holder. Next, cut the white paper to

fit inside the tree tag holder. You can write a message on the white paper, tuck it into the holder, and hang it on your tree.

Tree Tags

47

12th Night Cake

For colonial Virginians, New Year's Eve was not a night filled with parties, but Twelfth Night, usually celebrated on January 5, was. The next day was the Christian holiday of Epiphany and the end of the long holiday season. So the Twelfth Night party was the merriest of all, with dancing and feasting and card playing. The centerpiece of all the merrymaking was the cutting of the Twelfth Night cake.

Twelfth Night cakes were rich, made with eggs, butter, flour, almonds, currants, brandy, and candied pieces of orange and lemon. They may have been something like what we call fruit cakes, but there was no particular recipe, except for one special ingredient: a dried bean. The bean was the most important part of the recipe, because when the cake was cut, the person whose piece had the bean in it reigned as king of Twelfth Night. But the "king" also had to pay a price for the getting bean: hosting the Twelfth Night party the next year.

To make your own Twelfth Night cake, choose any recipe you like—it doesn't have to be anything like the colonial-style cake, or try the one on page 57. Just make sure it includes the special bean. But instead of a dried bean, which can be hard on the teeth, try using a jelly bean or a small piece of dried fruit. And make your cake the centerpiece of your own party, with games and songs and dancing and good cheer for the new year.

Trees are not the only recent additions to a Williamsburg Christmas. The wreath-making tradition begun by townspeople in the 1930s is still celebrated. Today, natural materials as well as colonial-era items are used in the wreaths, and that has led to amazing creations decorated with everything from oyster shells to okra pods, from clay pipes to playing cards. Just as in the early years of the town's restoration, prizes are still given for the most imaginative wreaths.

No doubt the old colonial Virginians would be amazed to visit their town these days in December. They'd certainly feel right at home with much of what they saw, but some things would surprise them. And what might surprise them most is that after more than 200 years, so many people want to visit Williamsburg at Christmas, to see and enjoy the very things they enjoyed at the holidays. We all take our own lives and traditions a little bit for granted, but who knows, maybe centuries from now, people will want to re-create some of the ways we celebrate Christmas. After all, each of us is making history and creating traditions in our own life even while we live it.

BELOW: Blazing cressets are the only lights along Duke of Gloucester Street, Colonial Williamsburg's main thoroughfare, their glow conjuring a bygone era.

Decorate Your Own
Wreath

The doors of many historic houses in Colonial Williamsburg are decorated with imaginative wreaths. People use all kinds of natural ingredients on their wreaths, from fruits and nuts to dried seedpods, berries, and pinecones. Try thinking of natural ingredients you might use to decorate your own wreath, especially things that grow in your area. Here's how you can attach simple things to a wreath to make a great door decoration.

6 Now place your decoratio around the wreath so the look festive. To secure ea decoration, push the flora pick under the wire frame that is holding the evergreens. Experiment with designs and ingredients. You'll be surprised how g it feels to see your own hand-decorated wreath hanging on your front do

1 You'll need a wreath (you can buy real evergreen ones at many stores during the holidays), scissors, green pipe cleaners, thin green floral wire and floral picks (both available in craft shops), and your choice of natural decorations. Cones and berries make nice seasonal touches and they're easy to attach.

 2 Cut the berry twigs so they're only four to five inches long, and trim off any leaves.

 3 Put four or five twigs together, enough so that you have a colorful bunch. Next take a floral pick, hold it close to the twigs, and wrap the wire tightly around the floral pick and the twigs to make a little berry bouquet. Make as many bouquets as you'd like, but six or seven looks nice on a wreath.

 4 Wrap each bouquet with a green pipe cleaner. Start right below the berries and wrap the pipe cleaner to the end of the floral pick. The green pipe cleaner will blend in with the color of the wreath when you attach the berry bunches.

 5 For the pinecones, hold a floral pick about one inch from the bottom of the cone and wrap wire tight around the cone and the pick. Five pinecones is a good number to decorate a wreath.

51

An American CHRISTMAS

CHRISTMAS IN WILIAMSBURG is a magical experience. No other place offers such a joyous celebration of the present along with a powerful and carefully created connection to the past. Why is Christmas in Williamsburg so special today? After all, as this book illustrates, the colonial Christmas wasn't such a big deal. Church, dinner, dancing, some evergreens, visiting—that was pretty much it.

In a way, it all started in 1934, not long after the beginning of the restoration of the Historic Area. A landscape architect named Arthur Shurcliff suggested placing a single lighted candle in each of the windows of the few buildings then open to the public. He remembered his family had followed this tradition in Boston. Louise Fisher, who was in charge of flowers in the Historic Area, decorated the doors and windows of the Palace and the Raleigh Tavern with fresh greenery.

The decorations caught on, not only in Williamsburg but throughout the country, especially when electric candles replaced real ones so people didn't have to worry about setting the house on fire.

Today Christmas in Williamsburg is celebrated with not just candles but also fireworks, and the simple greenery has evolved into elaborate decorations made from fresh fruits, vegetables, and evergreens. It is a grand celebration that large crowds of enthusiastic guests enjoy annually.

Why does this Williamsburg Christmas resonate so much? And why should you wish to capture the spirit of a Williamsburg Christmas for your own home? Well, perhaps, Christmases of old seem purer, less materialistic, and therefore more imbued with Christmas spirit. Bringing a Williamsburg Christmas to your home means more time spent making food, creating decorations, and learning customs, and less time buying gifts. Today's Williamsburg Christmas evolved from the traditions of the past and succeeds in capturing a truly timeless spirit. It is the epitome of an American Christmas.

— *Emma Lou Powers, Historian, The Colonial Williamsburg Foundation*

LEFT: Christmas is a time of warm welcomes.

Festive RECIPES

Several of the following recipes are adapted from 18th-century recipes and will add the taste of tradition to any Christmas celebration. Kids, be sure to ask your parents for help in the kitchen.

Pink-Colored Pancakes

1 large red beet
⅓ cup sugar
4 egg yolks (or equivalent
   amount of egg substitute)
½ cup heavy cream
   (or you can use skim
   milk or low fat cream)
3 oz. brandy

½ freshly grated nutmeg
¾ cup all-purpose flour
Butter for frying (you may
   substitute margarine or oil)
Chopped preserved
   apricots or chopped
   pistachios, for garnish

Boil the beet with the skin on until tender. Let cool, then remove the skin with a paper towel. Roughly chop the beet and then puree it in a food processor. While the processor is running, add the sugar, egg yolks, cream, brandy, and nutmeg. Stop the processor from time to time to scrape down the sides. When everything is well pureed, add the flour to combine to a smooth batter. Heat a nonstick frying pan to medium heat and melt a small amount of butter in the pan. Spoon ¼ cup of the mixture for each pancake into the pan and fry on both sides until done. Repeat until all the batter is used up. Garnish with preserved apricots or pistachios.

Chicken the French Way

1 whole chicken
¼ cup bread crumbs
1 tsp. parsley, minced
2 cups chicken broth
4 cups white wine
1 medium onion, diced
1 shallot, diced

½ cup golden raisins or grapes
Juice of 1 lemon
3 egg yolks (or you may thicken
   with 1 Tbsp. cornstarch and ½
   cup water, stir it well, and add it
   to cook for the last 5 minutes)

Cut the chicken into four parts. Coat lightly with bread crumbs and parsley. Over low to medium heat, broil or grill 5–7 minutes or until lightly brown, but the meat is still pink by the joints. Place chicken in a stewpot with broth, wine, onion, shallot, raisins or grapes, and lemon juice. Simmer for 25 minutes; remove chicken. In a medium bowl, whip the egg yolks. Gradually add ¼ cup of the sauce to the yolks while stirring to temper the eggs. Stir mixture into the rest of the sauce. Heat gradually until sauce thickens. Pour sauce over the chicken and serve.

Carrot Pudding

½ lb. carrots, scraped
1 lb. bread crumbs
1 whole fresh nutmeg, grated
4 eggs plus 4 yolks
1 cup sugar
1 cup cream (may use skim milk or
  low fat cream or evaporated milk)

½ lb. unsalted butter,
  melted (optional)
3 tsp. orange-flower water
1 cup cream sherry
Puff pastry for a 9-inch
  pie pan

Preheat the oven to 350°F. Grate the carrots into a bowl. Add the bread crumbs and nutmeg and stir to combine. In another bowl, using an electric mixer, mix the eggs, sugar, cream, melted butter, orange-flower water, and sherry until smooth. Pour the egg mixture into the carrot mixture and stir to combine. Line a 9-inch pie pan with puff pastry. Pour in the mixture and bake in the oven 35–40 minutes, until set. When done, allow it to cool to room temperature before serving.

Sugar Cookies

¼ cup unsalted butter
¼ cup shortening
1 cup sugar
1½ tsp. grated orange peel
1 tsp. vanilla extract
1 egg

3 Tbsp. milk
2 cups sifted
  all-purpose flour
1 tsp. baking soda
¼ tsp. salt
2 tsp. cream of tartar

Cream the butter, shortening, and sugar. Stir in the orange peel and vanilla extract. Stir in the egg and milk. Sift the flour, baking soda, salt, and cream of tartar and add to the creamed mixture. Mix well. Roll into 1-inch balls and roll the balls in sugar. Arrange the balls 1½ inches apart on ungreased cookie sheets. Flatten the balls gently with a small glass. Bake in a preheated 350°F oven 8–10 minutes or until very light golden brown. (If you like, you can roll out the dough and use cookie cutters to make shapes such as the hearts above.)

Syllabub
(Syllabub is traditionally made with wine or sherry. This version has been adapted for kids.)

1½ cups whipping cream
Grated rind and juice of 2 lemons

½ cup sugar
⅔ cup ginger ale

Whisk the whipping cream by hand until it thickens a bit. Add the lemon rind, lemon juice, sugar, and ginger ale one at a time, whisking by hand after each addition. Whisk the mixture 3–5 minutes until thickened. Keep in mind that too much whipping will turn it into butter. Pour into dessert glasses and refrigerate overnight. The mixture will separate when it stands.

Gingerbread House Dough

1 cup sugar
2 tsp. ginger
1 tsp. nutmeg
1 tsp. cinnamon
½ tsp. salt
1½ tsp. baking soda

½ cup evaporated milk
1 cup unsulfured molasses
1 cup margarine, melted
4 cups stone-ground or
    unbleached flour, sifted

Combine the sugar, ginger, nutmeg, cinnamon, salt, and baking soda. Mix well. Add the melted margarine, evaporated milk, and molasses. Mix well. Add the flour 1 cup at a time, stirring constantly. The dough should be stiff enough to handle without sticking to fingers. Knead the dough for a smoother texture. Add up to ½ cup additional flour if needed to prevent sticking. When the dough is smooth, roll it out ¼ inch thick on a floured surface and cut desired shapes. Bake on floured or greased cookie sheets (or parchment-lined pans) in a preheated 375°F oven 10–12 minutes. The dough is done if it springs back when touched.

Royal Icing (Gingerbread House "glue")

3 egg whites   1 lb. powdered sugar   ½ tsp. lemon juice

Place all ingredients in a mixing bowl. Using a paddle beat to a stiff consistency. If the mixture is too soft, add more powdered sugar. If it is too thick, add a few drops of water.

CHRISTMAS
Time Line

Roman Era
Celebrations of Saturnalia, held in mid- to late December, include feasting, hunting, and other festivities.

Early Christian Era
Probably sometime in the fourth century, the Church of Rome adopts December 25 as the Feast of the Nativity, to celebrate the birth of Jesus. During the same period, Nicholas, later St. Nicholas, serves as a bishop in what is now Turkey.

7th Century
Christianity, and with it the Feast of the Nativity, reaches Britain.

9th Century
British law extends the Christmas season from 9 days to 12, ending on Twelfth Night, the day before the Christian celebration of Epiphany.

11th Century
The Old English term for the Festival of Christ, Christes Maesse, becomes widely used.

16th Century
Puritans in Britain strike Christmas and all the saint days from their calendar, keeping only the Sabbath as a holy day.

17th Century
Puritans in Massachusetts also ban Christmas, but in Virginia colonists follow British customs of feasting and visiting during the Twelve Days of Christmas. In New Amsterdam (now New York), Dutch colonists hold hearty celebrations with their own traditions.

Early 1800s
New York writer Washington Irving describes holiday traditions, including the

12th Night Cake

1 cup butter or margarine
3 Tbsp. orange juice concentrate
2 tsp. grated orange rind
½ tsp. vanilla
¼ tsp. salt
4 eggs, room temperature

4 egg yolks, room temperature
1 cup sugar
1½ cups flour, sifted
¼ cup cornstarch
Sifted powdered sugar

Combine butter, juice concentrate, rind, vanilla, and salt in a small saucepan; cook over low heat, stirring, until butter is melted. Remove from heat; cool to lukewarm. Place eggs, egg yolks, and sugar in a large bowl; beat until tripled in volume. Sprinkle flour and cornstarch over egg mixture. Add butter mixture; fold in very gently until there is no trace of butter mixture. Pour into greased 9-inch tube pan. Bake in preheated 350°F oven for about 40 minutes or until cake starts to come away from sides of pan. Cool. Remove from pan. Sprinkle top of cake with powdered sugar.

First three recipes from "History Is Served," http://recipes.history.org; Sugar Cookies recipe from *Recipes from the Raleigh Tavern* published by The Colonial Williamsburg Foundation in 1984; Syllabub recipe adapted from *The Williamsburg Cookbook* published by The Colonial Williamsburg Foundation (CWF) in 1971; Gingerbread House recipe from CWF; Twelfth Night Cake recipe adapted from www.azcakerecipes.com in consultation with CWF.

Dutch Sancte Claus, and the English customs of mistletoe and making merry.

1823
"A Visit from Saint Nicholas," now known as "The Night Before Christmas," appears anonymously in the *Troy Sentinel*, a newspaper in upstate New York. It is later credited to scholar and poet Clement Clarke Moore.

1840s
Christmas trees, a German tradition, begin to appear in Britain and America. Prince Albert, a German by birth and the husband of Britain's Queen Victoria,

decorates a tree in Windsor Castle, and the custom becomes popular. In America, German immigrants introduce the tradition.

1842
German professor Charles Minnigerode decorates Williamsburg's first Christmas tree in the St. George Tucker House.

1843
Charles Dickens's *A Christmas Carol* is published, and the first commercial Christmas cards are sold in America.

1862
Popular illustrator Thomas Nast draws a scene called

"Santa Claus in Camp," showing a round elf-like man passing out gifts to Union troops during the Civil War. In the next few decades, Nast's jolly, smiling elf becomes America's image of Santa Claus.

20th Century
Christmas becomes ever more popular in America. In mid-century, Hollywood filmmakers produce such enduring seasonal classics as *Miracle on 34th Street*, *It's a Wonderful Life*, and *White Christmas*. By the century's end the holiday season extends from Thanksgiving until New Year's Day.

RESOURCES

The Artfull Tree: Ornaments to Make Inspired by the Abby Aldrich Rockefeller Folk Art Museum, by Jan Gilliam and Christina Westenberger. The Colonial Williamsburg Foundation, 2011.

Author Unknown: Tales of a Literary Detective, by Don Foster. Holt Paperbacks, 2001.

Christmas in America: A History, by Penne L. Restad. Oxford University Press, 1996.

Christmas in Colonial Virginia, by Mary R. M. Goodwin. The Colonial Williamsburg Foundation, 1955.

Colonial Williamsburg Journal articles on Christmas. Searchable online through http://research.history.org/JDRLibrary/Online_Resources/search.cfm?resource=journal.cfm

The Journal and Letters of Philip Vickers Fithian, Hunter Dickinson Farish, ed. The Colonial Williamsburg Foundation, 1957.

The Sketchbook of Geoffrey Crayon, by Washington Irving. Kessinger Publishing, 2009.

A Visit from St. Nicholas, by Clement Clarke Moore. Shadow Mountain, 2009.

Williamsburg Christmas, by Harry Abrams, Libbey Hodges Oliver, and Mary Miley Theobald, Inc., in association with The Colonial Williamsburg Foundation, 1999.

Christmas Traditions from Across the Country:

The Grand Illumination, held the first Sunday of December, heralds the holiday season in Colonial Williamsburg. Seasonal activities continue through the New Year's holiday.

For much of the country, the Christmas season is ushered in by watching a broadcast of the Macy's Thanksgiving Day Parade, an 86-year-old tradition.

The National Christmas Tree on the Ellipse behind the White House has been a feature of the Capital's holidays for decades. Lighted in early December by the President, it is surrounded by other trees representing the states and territories of the United States of America.

The Christmas tree at Rockefeller Center in midtown Manhattan. Since 1931, when the first unofficial tree was put up here by construction workers, this tree has been the centerpiece of Christmas in New York.

More recipes from Colonial Williamsburg are available online at http://recipes.history.org/

Abby Aldrich Rockefeller Folk Art Museum, Williamsburg, Va. 45
Armonicas 44, **44**

Boxing Day 23
Bruton Parish Church, Williamsburg, Va. 38

Caroling 30, **30**
Christmas cards 11, 31, 57
A Christmas Carol (Dickens) 31, 57
Christmas Eve 18
Christmas trees
  candle decorations 27–28, **28**, 45, **56**
  Colonial Revival style **42**
  introduced in America (1840s) 57
  Regency style **8**
  tree tags **46**, 47, **47**
  Victorian ornaments **29, 31**
Civil War 31, 57
Clark, Frank **19**
Clove-covered oranges 24–25, **24–25**
College of William & Mary, Williamsburg, Va. 18, **18**, 27
Colonial Revival style **42**
Cookies 23, 41, 43, 45
  recipe 55
Cressets 41, **49**

Dancing 11, **20–21**, 28, 30, 41, **44–45**, 48, 52
Decorations, making
  gingerbread houses 39, **39**, 56
  paper chains 32–33, **32–33**
  pomanders 24–25, **24–25**
  tree tags 47, **47**
  wreaths 50–51, **50–51**
Dessert pyramids 20, 43, **43**, 45
Dickens, Charles 31, 37, 57
Diehl, Rodney 39

Duke of Gloucester Street, Williamsburg, Va. 18, 39, 41, **49**

Epiphany 48, 56
Evergreen boughs 10, 37

Feast of the Nativity 56
Fife and drum corps **34–35**, 39, 41
Fireworks 11, 39, **40**, 52
Fisher, Louise 52
Fithian, Philip 17–18, 20
Fox hunting 11, 17, **23**
Franklin, Benjamin 44
Fruit pyramids 43, **43**, 45

German immigrants 11, 27, 57
Gilded nuts 27, 45
Gingerbread houses 39, **39**
  dough recipe 56
Governor's House, Williamsburg, Va. 41, 52
  gingerbread house **39**
  kitchen **19**
Grand Illumination 11, 39, **40**, 58

Holly 10, 18, 37, 38
Hot chocolate 19, **19**
Hymns 28, 30

Irving, Washington 56

Jamestown, Va. 15
Jefferson, Thomas 20
Jesus Christ 10, 56

Kissing balls 20, **20**

Minnigerode, Charles 27–28, 31, 57
Mistletoe 10, 57
Moore, Clement Clarke 30, 57
Music 11, 30, 41, 44
Muskets, firing of **18**

Nast, Thomas 27, 31, 57
  illustration by **26**
New Year's Day 23
New York Sun (newspaper), letter in **29**
Nicholas, Saint 11, 30, 31, 56
  see also Santa Claus
"The Night Before Christmas" (poem) 11, 27, 28, **29**, 30, 57

Oranges
  fruit displays 43, **43**, 45
  pomanders 24–25, **24–25**

Paper chains 32–33, **32–33**, 45
Pilgrims **14**, 15
Pineapples 11, **11**, 38, 45
Plantations 15, 17, 20
Pomanders 24–25, **24–25**
Puritans 15, 56

Raleigh Tavern, Williamsburg, Va. 52
Recipes
  Carrot Pudding 55
  Chicken the French Way 54
  Gingerbread House Dough 56
  Hot Chocolate 19
  Pink-Colored Pancakes 54
  Royal Icing 56
  Sugar Cookies 55
  Syllabub 55
  Twelfth Night Cake 48, 57
Regency style **8**, 47
Rockefeller, John D., Jr. 37, 42
Roman era 56

Santa Claus
  popular image **26**, 27, 31, 57

tree ornaments **29, 31**
Shurcliff, Arthur 52
Slaves **16**, 17, 20, 22, **22**
Smith, Captain John 15
Songs and singing 30, 48
Spicy decorations. *see* Pomanders
St. George Tucker House, Williamsburg, Va. 28, **32**, 45, 57
Sweetmeats 43
Syllabub 41
  recipe 55

Table settings 20, 42–43, **43**
Time line 56–57
Tree ornaments **29, 31**, 38, 45
Tree tags **46**, 47, **47**
Troy Sentinel (newspaper) 30, 57
Tucker family 27–28
Twelfth Night cake 48, **48, 57**
  recipes 48, 57
Twelve Days of Christmas 11, 13, 17, 18, 20, 23, 42, 43, 56

Victorian era 27–31
  caroling 30
  tree ornaments **29, 31**

Washington, George 20
Wassailing 30
Weddings 20, **20–21**
White Lighting 39
Williamsburg, Va.
  as colonial capital 17, 37
  first Christmas tree (1842) 11, 27–28, 32, 45, 57
  restoration (1930s) 11, 37–38, 42, 49, 52
Williamsburg Inn, Williamsburg, Va. **8, 46**, 47
Wreath, decorating your own 50–51, **50–51**

Illustrations Credits

All photographs copyright © 2011 Lori Epstein, www.loriepstein.com, unless otherwise noted below.

Special thanks to David M. Doody at Colonial Williamsburg for the following photos: 28-29, 30, 34-35, 38, 44 (bottom left), 45, 48 (top), 49, 54 (top), 55 (top and bottom).

14, original artwork by Howard Pyle/North Wind Picture Archives; 20 (inset), aceshot1/Shutterstock; 22 (bottom right), Stockbyte/Getty Images; 23 (top center), Justin Locke/National Geographic Vintage/Corbis; 24 (center), Nicholas Piccillo/Shutterstock; 26, original artwork by Thomas Nast/Bettmann/Corbis; 29 (top left), 31 (top left), courtesy Dresden Star Ornaments/www.victorianornaments.com; 29 (right), courtesy Newseum; 38, Seleznev Valery/Shutterstock; 50, Madlen/Shutterstock; 54 (bottom), Tom Green/Colonial Williamsburg; 54 (wooden spoon), Stephen Aaron Rees/Shutterstock; red Christmas ornament used throughout, scphoto60/Shutterstock

To my husband, Buzz, and son, Will, for so many happy Christmases—KMK
To Kate, Sophie, Alex, and Kiera for spicing up the holidays and every day! —LE

Colonial Williamsburg's cast of hundreds of professionals made this book possible—my thanks to them all. And special thanks to Paul Aron, Managing Editor of Publications, for his guidance and support for this project; Jae White, Manager of Historic Area Program Support; and Barbara Tyler-Mullins, Program Coordinator, who worked tirelessly to make all the elements come together into an historically accurate picture. Also thanks to Michelle Brown, Frank Clark, Rodney Diehl, Dave Doody, James Gay, Tom Green, Tom Hammond, Brian Lambert, Barbara Lombardi, Emma L. Powers, Sherri Powers, Kathy Rose, Laura Viancour, and the Walker family for preserving and celebrating the traditions of Christmas in Williamsburg. And to my own National Geographic team (Jennifer Emmett, Jim Hiscott, and Lori Epstein) for sharing the holiday spirit and their love of book-making with me. —KMK

The Colonial Williamsburg Foundation also appreciates the help of following models who participated in re-creating historic scenes: Great Hopes Plantation—Robert Watson, Sam Wilson, Brandon Hewitt, Kathleen Getward, Micah Canaday, Nyla Holiday, and Malan House; Making pomanders—Claire Mackert and Mattie Goad; Making paper chain—Alexander Boscana and Rachel Glasgow; Enslaved women cooking—Hope Smith, Janine Harris, and Keonte Holiday; Boxing Day—David Arehart and Keonte Holiday; Dinner and wedding—Donna Wolf, Doris Warren, Ron Warren, Brett Walker, Levi Walker, Zipporah Walker, Annaiah Walker, Benjamin Walker, Elita Walker, Sarah Woodyard, Jared Lorio, Jack Flintom, Amy Griffin, Joe Ziarko, Valerie Chapman, Justin Chapman, and Herb Watson; 1940s Christmas—Neal Hurst, Al Saguto, Karen Schlicht; Wreath making—Wilhelmina Grow and Truman Boyd; Firing Christmas guns—Tom DeRose, Cameron Butler, Andrew Swanson, Sharon Hollands, Sophie Lancione, and Ken Briner; Barring out—Andrew Kersey, Alec Gilliam, Chris Hochella, John Shideler, and Todd Norris. And to the following for their help in assuring the authenticity of these scenes—Regina Blizzard, Terry Lyons, Betty Myers, Debbie Mitchell, Rachel Merkley, Kevin Ernst, Rob Brantley, and Cynthya Nothstine.

Published by the National Geographic Society
John M. Fahey, Jr., *Chairman of the Board and Chief Executive Officer*
Timothy T. Kelly, *President*
Declan Moore, *Executive Vice President; President, Publishing*
Melina Gerosa Bellows, *Executive Vice President; Chief Creative Officer, Books, Kids, and Family*

Prepared by the Book Division
Nancy Laties Feresten, *Senior Vice President, Editor in Chief, Children's Books*
Jonathan Halling, *Design Director, Books and Children's Publishing*
Jay Sumner, *Director of Photography, Children's Publishing*
Jennifer Emmett, *Editorial Director, Children's Books*
Carl Mehler, *Director of Maps*
R. Gary Colbert, *Production Director*
Jennifer A. Thornton, *Managing Editor*

Staff for This Book
Jennifer Emmett, *Project Editor*
James Hiscott, Jr., *Art Director, Designer*
Lori Epstein, *Senior Illustrations Editor*
Kate Olesin, *Editorial Assistant*
Kathryn Robbins, *Design Production Assistant*
Hillary Moloney, *Illustrations Assistant*
Grace Hill, *Associate Managing Editor*
Sam Bardley, *Interim Associate Managing Editor*
Lewis R. Bassford, *Production Manager*
Susan Borke, *Legal and Business Affairs*

Manufacturing and Quality Management
Christopher A. Liedel, *Chief Financial Officer*
Phillip L. Schlosser, *Senior Vice President*
Chris Brown, *Technical Director*
Nicole Elliott, *Manager*
Rachel Faulise, *Manager*
Robert L. Barr, *Manager*

The National Geographic Society is one of the world's largest nonprofit scientific and educational organizations. Founded in 1888 to "increase and diffuse geographic knowledge," the Society works to inspire people to care about the planet. National Geographic reflects the world through its magazines, television programs, films, music and radio, books, DVDs, maps, exhibitions, live events, school publishing programs, interactive media and merchandise. *National Geographic* magazine, the Society's official journal, published in English and 33 local-language editions, is read by more than 38 million people each month. The National Geographic Channel reaches 320 million households in 34 languages in 166 countries. National Geographic Digital Media receives more than 15 million visitors a month. National Geographic has funded more than 9,400 scientific research, conservation and exploration projects and supports an education program promoting geography literacy.

For more information, please call 1-800-NGS LINE (647-5463) or write to the following address:
National Geographic Society
1145 17th Street N.W.
Washington, D.C. 20036-4688 U.S.A.
Visit us online at www.nationalgeographic.com/books
For librarians and teachers: www.ngchildrensbooks.org
More for kids from National Geographic: kids.nationalgeographic.com

For information about special discounts for bulk purchases, please contact National Geographic Books Special Sales: ngspecsales@ngs.org
For rights or permissions inquiries, please contact National Geographic Books Subsidiary Rights: ngbookrights@ngs.org

Library of Congress Cataloging-in-Publication Data
Kostyal, K. M., 1951-
 Christmas in Williamsburg : 300 years of family traditions / by K.M. Kostyal with the Colonial Williamsburg Foundation.
     p. cm.
 Includes index.
 1. Christmas–Virginia–Williamsburg–History. 2. Williamsburg (Va.)–Social life and customs. I. Colonial Williamsburg Foundation. II. Title.
GT4986.V8K67 2011
394.266309755'4252–dc22
                                2011011797
Hardcover ISBN: 978-1-4263-0867-3
Reinforced Library Binding ISBN: 978-1-4263-0868-0

Printed in China
11/CCOS/1

Text copyright © 2011 K. M. Kostyal
Compilation copyright © 2011 National Geographic Society
Published by the National Geographic Society. All rights reserved.
Reproduction of the whole or any part of the contents without written permission from the publisher is prohibited.